COPYRIGHT & GENERAL DISCLAIMER:
OSTARA: THE SPRING EQUINOX
ALL TEXT AND IMAGES © 2017-2025 BOOK OF SHADOWS LLC, AMY CESARI

THIS BOOK DOES NOT CONTAIN MEDICAL ADVICE AND DOES NOT INTEND TO TREAT OR DIAGNOSE MEDICAL OR HEALTH ISSUES. ALWAYS SEEK PROFESSIONAL MEDICAL TREATMENT. AND DON'T EAT OR USE PLANTS IF YOU DON'T KNOW WHAT THEY ARE.

ALL RIGHTS RESERVED. For personal use only. No parts of this book may be reproduced, copied, or transmitted in any form, by any means, including photocopying, recording, or other electronic or mechanical methods, without the prior written permission of the author, except in the case of brief quotations for critical reviews and certain other noncommercial uses permitted by copyright law. **DISCLAIMER OF LIABILITY:** This book is for informational and entertainment purposes only and is not intended as a substitute for medical, financial, spiritual, or life advice of any kind. Like any craft involving flames, the power of your mind unhinged, eating plants and herbs, and the unyielding forces of the universe, Witchcraft poses some inherent risk. The author and publisher are not liable or responsible for any outcome of magical spells performed from this book or otherwise. Readers agree to cast spells, work with fire, ingest herbs, soak in bath salts, light candles and incense, channel deities, use spirit boards, and perform any and all other magical practices at their own risk. The images in this book are for decorative purposes—they are not realistic guides for arranging flame-based altars. Always place a fireproof dish beneath candles & incense. Leave clearance above & around flames. Do not place flammable objects near flames and never leave flaming things or incense unattended. Readers of this book take full responsibility when using fire. Readers accept full personal risk and responsibility for the outcome, consequence, and magic of any spells they cast. This book is not for children. And so it shall be.

This Book Belongs To:

What is Ostara?

Ostara is a celebration of the spring equinox—the astronomical first day of spring, when the tilt of the Earth aligns so day and night are of equal length.

Symbolically, this equinox represents balance, renewal, and a reawakening of nature and life after winter. It's a potent time for planting seeds (physical and magical) and inviting new beginnings.

Ostara is most often celebrated on March 20 or 21, though the exact astronomical time and day shifts slightly each year (approximately March 19–22 in the Northern Hemisphere, and September 19–22 in the Southern Hemisphere, where the seasons are opposite.)

THE WHEEL OF THE YEAR

The Wheel of the Year is a framework of seasonal energy. You can use this Wheel as a source of natural magic, attuning to the rhythms of the seasons to enhance your life and work in flow with nature.

The Wheel of the Year reminds us that every season of growth has a balancing season of rest, and that darker phases are essential parts of life alongside the light.

And keep in mind that these energies are guides, not rules. You can cast a spell whenever you need to. You don't have to wait for a specific season or moon phase. However, the Wheel of the Year can be a powerful tool and guidepost for your rituals and life. Use it as it calls to you.

Here's an overview of the eight sabbats on the Wheel of the Year, their approximate dates, and how they correspond to cycles of the moon.

While the seasons and the sun embody outer, active energy, the moon reflects inner, emotional energy. Moon cycles are shorter (about 28 days compared to a full year), so they're useful for shorter-term intentions. Both the sun and moon move from dark to light and back again—just as we do in the seasons of our lives.

IMBOLC: February 1 or 2. Imbolc is the time to celebrate the first signs of spring or the return of the sun's increasing light. This sabbat corresponds to the waxing crescent moon.

OSTARA: March 19-22. This sabbat is celebrated on the spring equinox. Witches often mark this day with a ritual planting of seeds. Ostara corresponds to the first quarter moon.

BELTANE: May 1. Beltane is a time for rituals of growth, creation, and taking action to make things happen. This sabbat corresponds to the waxing gibbous moon.

LITHA: June 20-22. This sabbat celebrates the summer solstice, when the sun is at its strongest. Litha is a time of great magical and personal power and corresponds to the full moon.

LUGHNASADH: August 1. This day is a celebration of the "first harvest" where we gather early grains, herbs, fruits, and vegetables from the earth. It corresponds to the waning gibbous moon, where light and power begin to descend from their fullest stage.

MABON: September 19-22. Celebrated on the autumnal equinox, this sabbat is about release, balance, and letting go. It is the second harvest and corresponds to the last quarter moon.

SAMHAIN: October 31. Samhain is a celebration of the dark half of the year. It is a time to cast spells of protection for the upcoming winter. Samhain corresponds to the waning crescent moon.

YULE: December 20-22. Marked by the winter solstice and the shortest (darkest) day of the year, this sabbat corresponds to the dark and new moon.

A NOTE ABOUT THE SABBAT DATES: The dates for the two solstices and two equinoxes each year—Ostara, Litha, Mabon, and Yule—are calculated astronomically from the position of the Earth to the sun, so the dates given above are approximated. The "cross-quarter" festivals, which are the points between —Imbolc, Beltane, Lughnasadh, and Samhain—are commonly celebrated on "fixed" dates instead of the actual midpoints.

You might like to look up the exact dates each year, or you may prefer to keep it loose. It's the intention that counts, so choose the date that works best for you.

A NOTE ABOUT SOUTHERN HEMISPHERE SEASONS: If you're on the "southern" half of the Earth, like in Australia, the seasonal shifts are opposite. So you'll feel the energy of the summer solstice (corresponding to the full moon) in December instead of June.

-A HIGH LEVEL & HAND-WAVY-
HISTORY
OF OSTARA
& THE SPRING EQUINOX

Ostara is a modern witch's celebration of the spring equinox. Day and night are equal in length, and the sun's growing strength signals the return of spring.

For our ancestors, this was not just a seasonal change. It signals a turn of fate, as the scarcity of winter shifts towards the abundance of summer and the growth of new crops.

Spring has long been a time of feasts and rituals. Fields and gardens are prepared, seeds are planted, and households are cleansed to welcome fresh energy. Dairy foods, fresh greens, and eggs—all scarce in winter—return to the table as symbols of nature's renewal. Fertility is abundant and noticeable in sprouting plants, newborn animals, and the renewed vitality of the land.

Though the names, customs, and traditions differ, people have celebrated the spring equinox as a powerful time of renewal for thousands of years.

Scholars have often debated the origins of Ostara and how or if it connects to Easter. The name "Ostara" is commonly linked to the Anglo-Saxon goddess Ēostre, associated with dawn, fertility, and the returning light. While historical evidence of her worship is debated, her symbolism is powerful.

If you enjoy working your magic with historical accuracy, research and follow that desire. Yet, it's just as significant to celebrate Ostara with a focus on your lived experience and personal symbolism.

Explore Ostara as it calls to you, and the mystery and magic will unfold.

– A HIGH LEVEL & HAND-WAVY –
HISTORY
OF OSTARA
& THE SPRING EQUINOX

Spring equinox traditions around the world share similar themes and intentions.

Ostara is a powerful and liminal time, a doorway between dark and light, winter and spring, death and rebirth. It is also a moment of balance, suspended between past and future.

In Persia, Nowruz—the festival of the new year—honors rebirth with fire rituals, home cleansing, and offerings of greenery.

In Japan, Shunbun no Hi is a time for honoring ancestors and viewing the first cherry blossoms of the season.

European folk customs include blessing fields and wells, decorating eggs as fertility spells, and invoking good fortune.

Ancient people also observed the equinox through the sky itself. Monuments and sacred sites across the world, like the Maya city of Chichen Itza and the sacred stone circles in the British Isles, align with the sun's position at the equinox. These astronomical markers reveal how vital the sun and seasons were to agricultural societies.

As centuries passed and cultures evolved, springtime rites merged with new practices, yet the same themes endure. The desire to welcome warmth, celebrate growth, honor the renewal of life, and look forward to new opportunities has not changed.

Ostara invites us to honor the powers of the sun, and to reflect on what we wish to grow.

LEGENDS OF DAWN

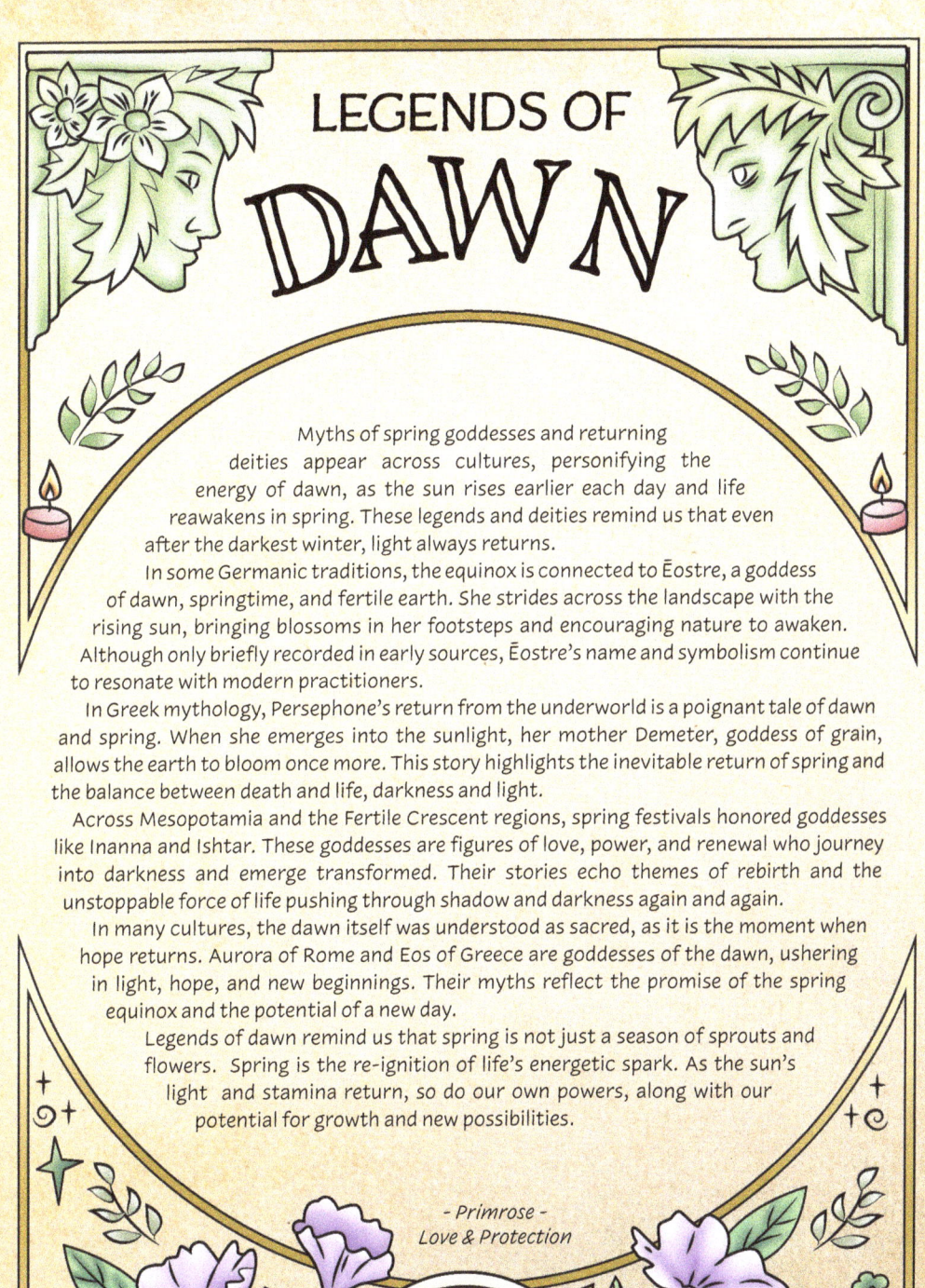

Myths of spring goddesses and returning deities appear across cultures, personifying the energy of dawn, as the sun rises earlier each day and life reawakens in spring. These legends and deities remind us that even after the darkest winter, light always returns.

In some Germanic traditions, the equinox is connected to Ēostre, a goddess of dawn, springtime, and fertile earth. She strides across the landscape with the rising sun, bringing blossoms in her footsteps and encouraging nature to awaken. Although only briefly recorded in early sources, Ēostre's name and symbolism continue to resonate with modern practitioners.

In Greek mythology, Persephone's return from the underworld is a poignant tale of dawn and spring. When she emerges into the sunlight, her mother Demeter, goddess of grain, allows the earth to bloom once more. This story highlights the inevitable return of spring and the balance between death and life, darkness and light.

Across Mesopotamia and the Fertile Crescent regions, spring festivals honored goddesses like Inanna and Ishtar. These goddesses are figures of love, power, and renewal who journey into darkness and emerge transformed. Their stories echo themes of rebirth and the unstoppable force of life pushing through shadow and darkness again and again.

In many cultures, the dawn itself was understood as sacred, as it is the moment when hope returns. Aurora of Rome and Eos of Greece are goddesses of the dawn, ushering in light, hope, and new beginnings. Their myths reflect the promise of the spring equinox and the potential of a new day.

Legends of dawn remind us that spring is not just a season of sprouts and flowers. Spring is the re-ignition of life's energetic spark. As the sun's light and stamina return, so do our own powers, along with our potential for growth and new possibilities.

- Primrose -
Love & Protection

LEGENDS
OF BALANCE & TRANSFORMATION

The spring equinox is a moment of balance when light and dark are perfectly matched and the world stands in equilibrium. Myth and folklore often describe this time as a threshold where transformation happens and opposites trade places. At Ostara, change is certain: ice melts, seeds crack open, and life begins to shift from possibility into becoming.

In Norse folklore, this balance is told in the story of Idunn, keeper of the apples of youth. When she's taken away, the gods begin to age and weaken. But when she is returned, they become young and vital again. Her myth symbolizes the contrast of youth and aging, and the cyclical nature of life and death.

In Egyptian mythology, the goddess Ma'at is a personification of truth and balance. She weighs the hearts of the dead against a feather. This sacred act shows balance and harmony between worlds: not too heavy, not too light. Her presence at the equinox evokes the clarity needed to choose what to carry forward and what to release as the seasons shift.

Snakes emerging from their winter dens represent personal and spiritual transformation. And as snakes shed their skin, they reveal brighter, stronger versions of themselves.

Frogs and toads undergo metamorphosis as well, moving between water and land, a living symbol of adapting to new ways of being.

These legends show us that change is a natural part of the cycle, and that balance does not deny transformation; it prepares you for it.

When the light of spring returns, take it as a sign from your intuition. It's time to grow beyond the old forms that once kept you safe. You can cross the threshold, renewed.

If you find a shed snakeskin, consider using it in a spell for transformation. Place it in a charm bag, set it on your altar, or burn it safely outdoors as a potent ritual offering.

Eat strawberries to manifest love and sweetness in life.

LEGENDS OF THE WILD

The natural world comes back to life in spring, as if by magic. The spring equinox represents balance, yet also potential. The life-force energy of nature is at a "tipping point" that can push you forward in new directions.

In British and Celtic folklore, the Green Man is a guardian of forests and new growth. His face appears in leaves and vines. He is the personification of nature and represents the vitality of the Earth. Each year, his spirit is reborn through the unfurling leaves, reminding us that nature is alive, powerful, and works in continual cycles of life, death, and rebirth.

Animals that emerge in spring carry symbols of their own. Rams and sheep, sacred in many pastoral cultures, symbolize protection, virility, and the flourishing of the flock. Their presence marks the end of winter and the promise of abundance. The sight of deer with fawns is an unmistakable sign that new life and energy have returned to Earth.

The hare is another symbol of the wildness of spring. In some folk traditions of Europe, hares are believed to transform into wise women or witches and are keepers of hidden knowledge and secrets of life.

Nature and wilderness are enchanted places in early spring. Forests, riverbanks, and blossoming fields are home to nature spirits and beings who guard sacred groves and spaces. In parts of Ireland and Scotland, offerings of milk or fresh herbs are left outdoors to acknowledge these spirits and ensure harmony with the wild.

Legends of the wild remind us that spring is not always gentle and sweet. It is an unstoppable surge of life, instinct, and untamed magic. As the earth awakens, so does the wild within us, calling us to explore, to grow, and to reclaim our connection to the magic of the wild and natural world.

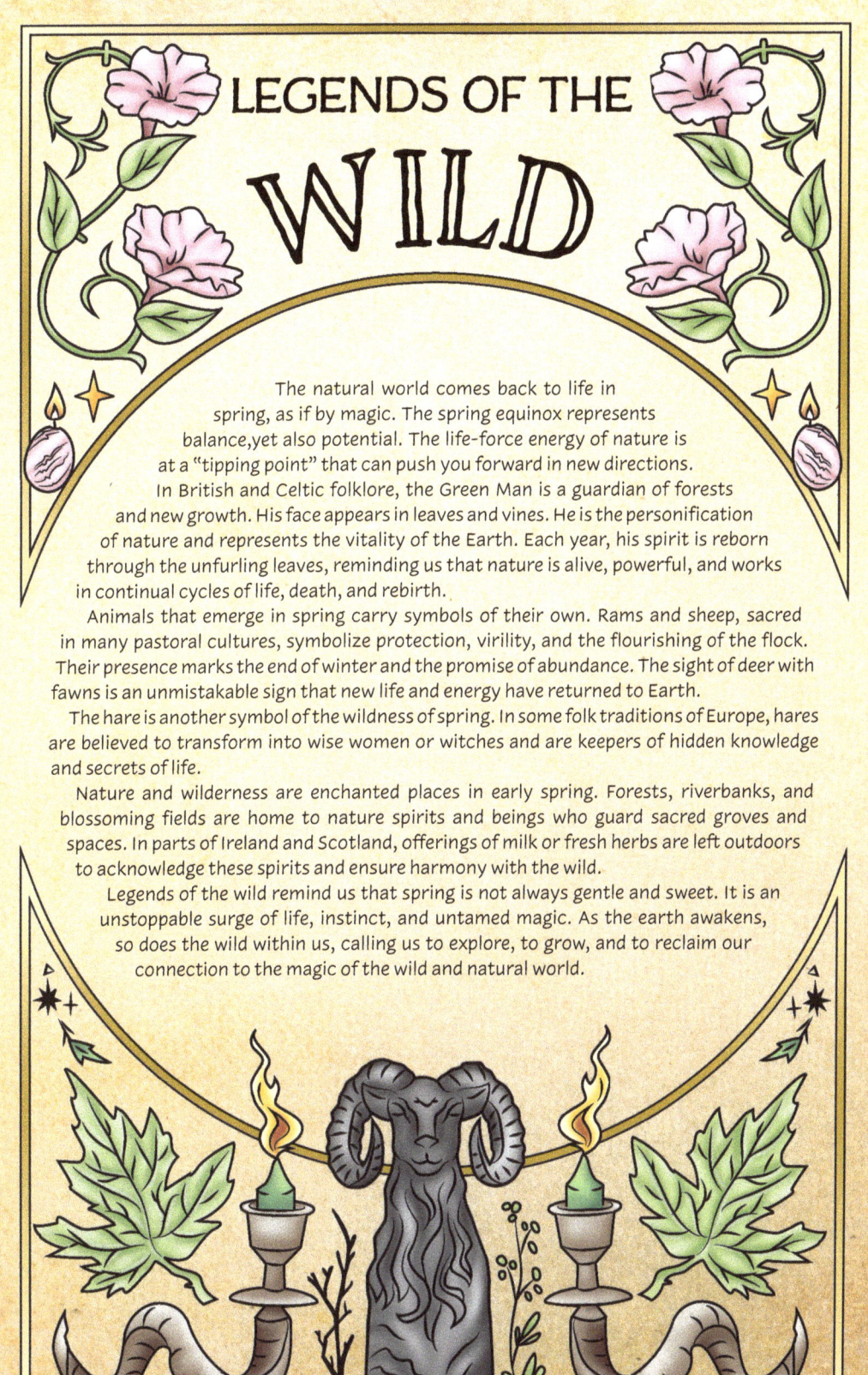

EDIBLE FLOWERS

Sprinkle edible flower petals like calendula, borage, pansy, and nasturtium onto your salads to bring the magic of the wild into your meal.

Moonstone and jasmine can help you cultivate self-love, clarity, and inner peace.

Music and sound are keys to the magical laws of the universe. Use music or sound to shift your energy.

If you find a raven's feather, wear it in your hat for energetic protection and witch power.

OSTARA SPELLS
AIR ELEMENT

Scent
Immerse yourself in the scent of fresh flowers or herbs.

Birds
Visit nature and observe birds. See how many you can count or search for feathers.

Laughter
Find reasons to laugh or listen to the laughter of babies & children.

Breeze
Open windows and let fresh air flow into your house.

Knowledge
Learn something new to bring fresh energy into your life.

Sunrise
Take a quiet walk or meditate at sunrise to set a peaceful tone for the day.

Make an elemental floor wash with sprigs of thyme (water), lavender (air), cloves (fire), and vetivert (earth).

Hold citrine to your heart or solar plexus to know your desires and inner wisdom.

Eat or burn basil leaves to gather courage.

Buy a bouquet of your favorite spring flower.

Creating an Ostara Altar
Centering Your Magical Focus and Intentions

Creating an altar is a powerful way to honor the spring equinox. An altar brings the spiritual into the material world—As Above, So Below—and becomes a place where intention takes form. The items you choose speak to your subconscious, stirring instinct, memory, and magic in ways deeper than language. Your Ostara altar is not just decoration—it's a living symbol of awakening, balance, and renewal.

To create an altar that reflects the energy of Ostara, gather a few items that evoke spring to you: early flowers, fresh herbs, eggs, crystals in pale or pastel colors, or symbols of dawn, growth, and new beginnings. You might also choose imagery connected to the season like hares, birds, sprouting seeds, the Green Man, or deities associated with spring.

Ask yourself a few guiding questions: What do I want to grow in my life this season? What forms of balance do I need? How do I want to feel? Let your answers guide what you place upon your altar.

For a more traditional altar setup, include representations of the goddess and god—perhaps a dawn or earth goddess paired with a solar or horned god. Add the four elements to call upon their powers—a candle for fire, a bowl of fresh water for the element of water, incense or a feather for air, and a stone, plant, or small dish of soil for earth.

But, remember, these are only suggestions. While inspiration comes from many places, the most meaningful altars arise from your own intuition. Choose colors, scents, symbols, and tools that reflect what awakens you, what nourishes you, and what invites you to begin again. Make your Ostara altar a place of renewal and reflection as the wheel turns to light.

Ostara Herbcraft
Spring Cleaning Rituals with Herbal Magic

Ostara is a time to clear away the heaviness of winter and create space for new beginnings. And spring cleaning can be a ritual and an invitation for fresh energy to return.

You don't need to clean your entire home. To begin, choose just one area that's been feeling neglected, cluttered, or frustrating, and focus your attention there.

Mint, rosemary, thyme, and other vibrant spring herbs are excellent for cleaning. Brew strong herbal teas and use them as floor washes, to wipe down doorways, or to cleanse the energy of your altar. Add lemon peel or a splash of vinegar to amplify clarity and renewal.

Herbal incense is another simple form of Ostara magic. Burn rosemary for clarity, garden sage for purification, or lemongrass for bright energy. Allow the smoke to drift into corners and across thresholds, carrying winter's stagnant energy away and refreshing your space with the scent of spring.

Simmer pots are perfect for Ostara. Place mint, basil, citrus slices, or other fresh herbs into a pot of water and let it steam gently on the stove. As the fragrance fills your home, visualize heaviness dissolving and new vitality flowing in.

Craft simple herb bundles and use them as altar brooms or symbolic spells. Tie dried rosemary, mint, or lavender with a bit of twine and hang it by your doorway or windows to welcome light, spring energy. Or tuck small sachets of thyme, chamomile, or basil into drawers and closets to refresh stagnant spaces.

And remember that Ostara herbcraft doesn't need to be elaborate to be powerful. A bouquet of freshly picked herbs or flowers will shift the energy of a room. As nature renews, feel into this spirit to renew yourself and your home, too.

Ostara Spells

Intention-Setting Ritual
Plant the Seeds for Your Magical Year

Ostara holds the most powerful seasonal energy to start new projects and phases in life.

1. THINK & FEEL: A few weeks before the Equinox, discover 1-3 things you want to manifest. Write them down. If you don't know the specifics, focus on the feeling that you want to experience, such as, "I want to feel fulfilled in life and excited to get out of bed," or "I want to feel like I'm part of a community."

If you're still not sure of what you want, check out some of the spells that follow in this book to explore a little deeper and find out.

2. PREPARE: Look up the day and time of the spring equinox for your time zone. Try and set aside 30 minutes at this time and day, but it does not have to be exact. Within a couple of days, or even a week, is fine.

3. FOR EACH MANIFESTATION:

- VISUALIZE: See and feel what you'd like through your third eye. Immerse yourself in the feeling of already having it in the present.

- MEDITATE: To deepen the feeling.

- VISUALIZE AGAIN: Bring your visualization to the lower back of your head and reflect on it again. If your neck gets tingly—awesome!

- Say "And so it shall be!" or "It is done."

4. REPEAT STEP 3 for each manifestation.

5. CLOSE: Take a few minutes to lock in all the positive feelings and intentions at the end.

6. TAKE ACTION: Let go of expectations and act in accordance by taking inspired action.

If you'd like to plant actual seeds to symbolize your intentions, do so after your ritual. As you tend to your seeds in the coming weeks, refresh the feeling, vision, and energy of what you intend to create.

"Mini" Manifestation Spells:

- Anoint a candle with olive oil and dried basil.
- Carry 7 coins in a bag with a sprig of cinquefoil.
- Tie nine knots in a green cord as you say and visualize your desire with each knot.
- Chop basil, dill, and parsley and use as a garnish.
- Burn bayberry candles with silver charms, chains, or coins surrounding them.

Ostara Spells

Manifestation Spellbox
A Spell to Symbolize Your Intentions

Ostara corresponds to the alchemical process of Separation—sifting, sorting, and deciding how you want to move forward. It is an excellent time to choose who you want to be in this next chapter of your life.

PREPARE: Reflect on who you desire to be or what you desire to have in this next phase of life. It may be good to do some soul-searching or journaling, but don't overthink it! Chances are, you already know what you want.

THINGS YOU'LL NEED: A cauldron or other fireproof place to burn paper. A small spell box or container—it could be a jar with a top, even an envelope will work. A pen, paper, and scissors.

CAST THE SPELL: Write down all of the "pieces of you"—past, present, and future, dark and light. Who are you? Who have you been? Who do you desire to be? Write it down.

Then, sort! Decide what you want to grow, and decide what you want to banish. If you want to banish something, burn it in the cauldron. If you want to grow something, put it in the manifestation spell box.

Once you've burned up all of the things you want to banish, sprinkle a little of the ashes over the things you want to grow. Close the box and consecrate it with flames, crystals, or incense.

Then, IMAGINE and FEEL your ideal vision. See and feel it through your third eye. Immerse yourself in the feeling of already having it.

Meditate to deepen the feeling. Then imagine it again, and bring the feeling to the lower back of your head. If your neck gets tingly—awesome!

Challenge yourself to feel hopeful, capable, and inspired for the entire day. Then act in accordance by taking inspired action towards what you envisioned.

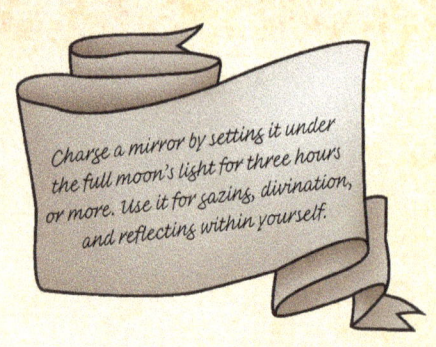

Charge a mirror by setting it under the full moon's light for three hours or more. Use it for gazing, divination, and reflecting within yourself.

Collect morning dew from Ostara to Beltane and use it in health & beauty potions

Shadows and Mirrors
Shining Spring's Light into the Dark

Periods of change and growth often involve sifting, sorting, analyzing, and making decisions based on your emotions and intuitive guidance.

This can help you figure out what you might desire for the future and guide you to set your spring intentions accordingly.

Mirrors and shadows work as opposites. Shadows block light, and mirrors reflect light. By reflecting light off a mirror and into the shadow, you can get a glimpse of what's going on in the darkness and integrate the shadows and light.

YOU'LL NEED: A mirror, scrying crystal, or a vessel of water to gaze into. A black (or other) candle to represent the unknown. A journal and pen. Tarot cards or another divination tool.

CAST THE SPELL: At midnight in a pitch-black room, place the black candle behind you and the mirror in front of you. Light the candle. Waft the smoke of visioning incense such as mugwort, cinnamon, or benzoin.

Ask to see into the shadows and unconscious mind, to bring them to rational light. Gaze into the mirror so you see the candle behind you. Think about the shadowy emotions, stories, and patterns that you've uncovered.

What shadows feel electric and alive? What magical parts of yourself have you been hiding or afraid of bringing to light? What shadows feel stagnant like a revolving door, a frustrating loop, or a trap? What are you ready to let go of? What's the sludge that's blocking your magic?

If you need clues, divine for answers using your tarot cards. Then bring it all to rational thought by writing about it in your journal.

Ostara Spells

Epic Broom Ride
A Journey To See Your Potential

On the spring equinox, journey through the veil of consciousness into whatever life you desire—in true witch style—on a broom.

The identity of "Witch" gives you the power to transform. This strength is especially potent at the spring equinox where seasonal energies are clambering to make things grow.

Prepare: Reflect on who you would be as your highest and best self. Picture it and write it down. (Dedicated! Contributing! Studious! Loving! Confident! Aligned with your best self!)

Things You'll Need: A ceremonial broom (optional). A cauldron of incense for visioning and dreams such as mugwort, rose, or angelica.

Cast the Spell: Sit comfortably with your broom nearby. Light your cauldron. Grasp the broom and close your eyes. If you're called to stand instead—do so. Say whatever words you desire, perhaps something like:

With the power of my mind's eye
Let me move forward, let this broom fly!

In the theatre of your mind, stride your broom and fling yourself up into the air. Shoot through time and space in whatever direction you like, into the future of you—your highest self.

Witness yourself flying over any obstacles or fears. You may see scenes or craggy black rocks beneath you. Fly over it, moving past at will.

Then, slow your broom and look down to see your highest self joyfully living the life of your dreams below you. Fly down and merge with this version of you.

Then, fly home with a renewed sense of self. Envision the route back to where you began. Open your eyes. Ground yourself, and make sure to write notes about what you saw on your broom ride, and who you became on the journey. Use this as your Ostara intention.

Ostara Spells

The Best Witch
A Bath Spell to Visualize Your Most Magical Self

Sometimes you have to get out of your own way to allow space for your intuition to be heard. The bath (or shower) is a powerful place to succumb to the element of water and your subconscious. It's a magical place for idea generation because it allows you to relax and let your true brilliance and guidance shine.

While you run your bath, light some candles and empowering incense, such as cinquefoil, frankincense, or bay. Place crystals like clear quartz or amethyst (to amplify your sense of self) and citrine (happiness) on the edges or in the water. Dump in 1/2 cup of salt and 1/4 cup of herbs for positive visions such as mugwort, rose, calendula, jasmine, and lemon.

Hold the intention to clear the static and shadow and allow your highest and best nature, new ideas, and best self to rise. If you are taking a shower, mix the salt and herbs with 1/2 cup of jojoba oil or shea butter to make a body scrub.

Get in the bath. As you're fully immersed in water, allow yourself to visualize your best self. Feel yourself as happy, successful, and fulfilled, abundant, or as peaceful as you want, in whatever ways that feel right.

Then relax and let your mind empty of all thoughts and visions, allowing silence or subconscious energy to arise and fill you with inspiration, new ideas, and a "next" level of yourself, your consciousness, and what you desire.

After your spell and for the next several days, take notes of any ideas or visions that came to you and use them to guide and deepen your intentions, actions, and spellwork going forward.

Burn or diffuse eucalyptus to clarify and release your emotions

Mix sea salts with crushed ash leaves and orange blossoms for a spiritually recharging bath or blessing water

Bath of Prophecies
A Sea Salt Spell to Channel Your Inner Guide

The sun shifts from Pisces to Aries at the spring equinox (in the northern hemisphere) and this energy is all about turning feelings into action.

ABOUT THE SPELL: We'll use Pisces magic to create a sea salt "Prophecy Powder." Use it as a bath salt or shower scrub, or to sprinkle on your tarot cards, spirit board, or other divination tool. We'll also make a delicious savory version that you can use for divinatory purposes in your cooking or kitchen spells. Then once you've received a prophecy or intuitive message with these tools, take inspired action towards it with "Aries" energy.

PREPARE YOUR PROPHECY SALTS: Mix 1/2 cup of quality sea salt and about 1/4 cup of dried herbs and petals (mugwort, jasmine, rose, and lavender are excellent herbs for visions). If you'd prefer a shower scrub, blend the herbs and salt with 1/2 cup of jojoba oil to create a paste.

Then cast a mystical bath environment with incense, candles, dim lighting, or whatever you desire. Sprinkle the bath salts into the hot water and submerge yourself. Allow your mind to drift to nothingness as you imagine yourself in the space between worlds. Then call a prophecy to appear to you from the celestial void. For the next several days, take note of any dreams, prophecies, or visions that come to you.

KITCHEN PROPHECIES: As an alternative to the bath spell, mix Celtic sea salt with dried bay, basil, and fennel seeds. Add chili powder for an extra kick. Keep it on your table and pull some tarot cards while you're in the kitchen—or sprinkle it on whatever you've got cooking—then divine for messages in the steam.

Ostara Spells

Magic Dream Sachet
A Spell to Learn From Your Dreams

Desiring change in the future brings up new questions and unknowns. Like, what's the next step?! First, trust that you likely already know the next step, and you only need to take one step at a time to make progress. It's okay to make change slowly or cautiously. You can also use the subconscious power of your dreams to give you some clues.

PREPARE: Gather materials to make a simple sachet or dream pillow. You can use a circle of fabric that you bundle up and tie with a string, or you can sew squares together nicely and make a little pillow. Your choice. Get the fabric, sewing supplies, and filling ready. For filling, you can use dried herbs, or you can use fabric scraps, crystals, and fewer herbs.

For herbs to enhance prophetic dreams, try mugwort, jasmine, and rose. Use bay, cinnamon, rowan, or yarrow to increase psychic powers. If you use oil, just use 1-2 drops.

DOING THE SPELL: Cast a Circle and Call the Quarters if you wish. Light a candle.

Place the fabric or pillow in front of you, and add the herbs, feeling the intention of each. Then, put it under your pillow. Before you go to bed, focus on the intention to have a dream that will tell you what to need to know, to awaken your creativity, to put you on the "right" path, or whatever you like.

Have a journal or paper ready to write down any dreams you have as soon as you wake up. If you don't have a dream that gives you clarity, that's okay. Keep your intuition open to signs and symbols that call to you when you're awake.

Elemental Action
Move Forward And Create Positive Change

In early spring, the turn of the seasons is unmistakable as the energy shifts to growth and new life. You can use this energy to create momentum by taking "inspired action" after setting your Ostara intentions.

At the first new moon after the Spring Equinox, or at any other new moon, start journaling, thinking, divining, and looking through these five "elemental lenses" listed below as a guide for your thoughts, questions, research, and action. You can focus on one per day, or you can reflect on a little bit of each as you feel called.

Take action and follow your intuition when you come up with exciting new ideas. Then keep rotating through all five of the elemental lenses, putting pieces together as you go, paying special attention to any coincidences, clues, intuitive flashes, good feelings, or patterns that arise.

Earth: What is my purpose and vision? What would I need to do to make my dreams real?

Air: What else do I need to learn? What's missing? How can I be more open to new information and insights?

Fire: How can I take action? How can I move things forward? What do I need to do to change, harness, or re-balance my energy?

Water: What feelings have I been avoiding? How can I use my emotions as guidance?

Spirit: How can I act in accordance with what is true to my heart and soul's purpose?

You might also want to try working with "Air" and "Fire" elements during the waxing moon phase, "Spirit" at the full moon, and "Water" and "Earth" during the waning moon phase, but that is entirely optional.

A Witch's Garden
Growing Your Magic on Earth and in Spirit

Spring bursts forth with a powerful and deeply spiritual essence of new life. It can feel awesome, yet also chaotic and unsettling, like the wild energy of the wind.

When we see growth on plants, it's exciting, but when it comes to personal growth, change can feel disjointing and unsure. In fact, the unconscious mind assumes "change" means "danger" and alerts you by creating anxiety... even if the "change" is something you want.

And so, you can use the "growth" energy of gardening (even just one small houseplant) to nurture yourself through changes. The energy of plants can help you shift your thoughts from the fears and doubts that often come with personal growth, to witnessing your magic, wonder, and progress instead.

Go as far into "gardening-as-witchcraft" as you like — plant trees, create an outdoor altar, labyrinth, pentagonal herb plot, an eight-pieced wheel, or an old cauldron filled with flowers.

Once you've planted your garden or anytime you see fit, have a candlelit procession or ceremony. Dedicate yourself to tend to the garden's well-being and growth as you go forth in your own personal development.

Then as you care for your plant(s) in the coming weeks, feel the energy of their growth. Watch them take root and witness the sense of sacred power that breathes life into all things. Feel that same power inside of yourself and visualize however you wish to be. In time, you'll naturally find that you connect to your highest self whenever you tend to your garden.

Ostara Tarot

WILL
What is my soul driven to do, have, or experience in life, no matter what?

EVOLUTION
What will lead me towards growth?

SPIRIT
What is my spirit guiding me towards that I fear or do not entirely trust?

Dandelion Root Tea
Manifesting through
Intuition

- Crescent Moon Scones -   - Nourishing Your Emotions -

*Charge your creative tools
under the full moon.*

Crafts for Ostara
Creating with the Beauty of Nature

Spring inspires creativity. As the first flowers bloom, Ostara invites us to craft with natural beauty of the season. These simple folk projects honor the spirit of rebirth, encourage connection to nature, and make charming gifts or additions to your altar or grimoire.

PRESSED FLOWERS: A classic Victorian craft that can be traced back as far as ancient Egypt, pressing flowers and herbs preserves the delicate beauty spring. Collect small blossoms, herbs, and leaves like violets, primrose, clover, mint, or whatever grows around you.

Press them between sheets of parchment and underneath heavy books for a week or two. Once dried, use them to decorate cards, spell pages, altar adornments, or as magical bookmarks.

BOTANICAL GRIMOIRE: Create a spring grimoire by pairing pressed flowers with notes about each plant: its magical properties, where you found it, or what it symbolizes to you. This becomes a personal herbarium—a record of your season and your magic. These pages make powerful keepsakes or gifts and can be used in spells for renewal or placed on your altar.

PAINTED ROCKS: Folk artists around the world paint stones for luck, protection, or blessings. Collect smooth rocks and decorate them with symbols of spring—eggs, hares, budding branches, runes, or spirals. Hide them in the garden as little blessings for the land, place them on your altar, or give them to friends as tokens of encouragement and renewal.

These sweet and simple crafts honor the season's energy and weave magic through your hands. Let your Ostara crafts be playful, gentle, and full of possibility—just like the season itself.

Ostara Intentions

Manifestation Crafts
Simple & Fun Spells For Growth

Manifestation Eggs are a fun and powerful spellcraft to do with kids, covens, or groups.

For each person, you'll need a blown-out egg, a small piece of paper and pen, a few seeds (something like wildflowers or sunflowers that are easy to sprout).

Write your intentions of what you wish to create or grow on a small piece of paper. Roll the paper up and stuff it into a blown-out egg. Add some seeds. Seal it with a small piece of masking tape. Decorate. Then, bury the egg, and as the flowers "hatch" as summer approaches, so shall your manifestations.

Manifestation Terrariums are another crafty way to enhance your Ostara rituals. You can make one with dirt and actual plants or succulents, or just fill up a jar with rocks, herbs, crystals, and other symbolic items.

Fill a small jar or earthen vessel with quartz pebbles (rose quartz, if you want to manifest love!) and any other meaningful accents of your choice: larger crystals, deity statues, notes, photographs, or herbs. Make sure to add things that are symbolic of what you want to manifest.

Recharge your terrarium as the year progresses by placing it under the full moon's light each month.

Anoint candles with rose and orange oil

Eggs & Tulips
New life, creation, and abundance

Celebrating Spring
Ancient Crafts for Abundant Blessings

The spring equinox holds the most powerful seasonal energy to start new projects and phases in life. So... who do you want to be? As a witch, you get to decide.

First make one of these crafts to signify your intentions, then use it in ritual to set your intentions for Ostara.

OSTARA EGGS: Ancient Persian cultures began the tradition of painting eggs thousands of years ago. Paint real eggs, paper eggs, or wooden ones. Use Persian Nowruz inspired designs or try Slavic Pysanka eggs painted with wax and color.

GOD POLES: Perhaps you'd prefer to carve a wooden deity statue, a "god pole" or ceremonial carving. Procure a balsa or basswood carving block, or clay if you prefer. Carefully carve or sculpt the image of your deity or guide.

PREPARE: A few days or weeks before the equinox, think deeply about who you want to be in this next cycle of life. Then write it down. (Dedicated! Loving! Confident! Aligned!)

Craft your eggs or god poles ahead of time to use as ritual tools and altar items or work the crafting process into your ritual if you prefer.

PERFORM THE RITUAL: Set up a meditative, magical space on the day or night of the equinox.

There are no specifics here, other than to IMAGINE or FEEL whatever it is you desire.

Feel it through your third eye and immerse yourself in the feeling of already having it.

Spend a few minutes to deepen the sensation, then bring the feeling to the lower back of your head. If your neck gets tingly—awesome.

Challenge yourself to stay inspired for the entire day or longer.

Natural Egg Dyes

Egg Crafts

Decorating eggs is a joyful and symbolic craft for Ostara. Eggs represent potential, renewal, and emerging life, so they're perfect vessels for magic. And working with natural dyes, herbs, and symbolism turns this simple folk craft into a meaningful ritual that honors spring's awakening.

Consider using natural dyes made from plants with magical energy. Simmer beets for deep pinks, turmeric for golden yellows, blueberries for blues and purples, red onion skins for earthy reds, spinach or parsley for greens, and coffee or black tea for browns. Research online for detailed instructions on how to create vibrant natural dyes.

Before dying your eggs, draw runes, sigils, or symbols with white crayon or wax. These hidden markings will resist the dye and reveal themselves afterward—a witchy way to add intention to your egg craft.

You can also wrap eggs in leaves, blossoms, or sprigs of herbs (like parsley, clover, or mint) before dyeing them. Bind tightly with cheesecloth or nylon stockings, then simmer them in dye to create botanical imprints—nature's art revealed on the shell.

After your eggs are dyed and dried, anoint them with a tiny drop of essential oil to further enchant their energy. Lemon or sweet orange brings joy and freshness; lavender brings calm and blessing; rosemary awakens clarity.

Your finished eggs can be placed on your Ostara altar, offered to the land, tucked into spring baskets, or given as gifts to bless friends with Ostara magic.

OSTARA POSTCARD

Copy onto heavy cardstock. Color, cut, and mail to your friends.
Finished Size: 4"x6".

- Tin -
Prosperity
& Elf Power

Spellcasting Basics

There are opening and closing steps that are basic accompaniments to spells in this book. These steps are optional but advisable: at least know "why" many witches perform these processes and try them out for yourself.

And keep in mind, this is a super basic "coloring book" guide to the spellcasting process. There are books and online sources that go much further in-depth.

THE SECRET OF SPELLS

The secret to powerful spells is in you. Your feeling and vibration in alignment with your true source of self—and/or a higher power—is what makes spells work.

The secret isn't in having the right ingredients and doing all the steps in a particular order. It's in your ability to focus your intent and use your feelings, mind, and soul to call in what you want—to harness the energy of yourself in harmony with the Earth, stars, moon, planets, or whatever other spiritual forces you call upon.

BREAK THE RULES

The first rule is to throw out any of the rules that don't work for you. Do things that feel right, significant, and meaningful. Adapt spells from different practices, books, and teachers. The only way to know what works is to follow your curiosity and try things out.

USING TOOLS

Your feelings and vibration are what unlocks the magic, not the tools, exact words, or sequences. You can cast amazing spells for free with no tools at all, and you can cast an elaborate spell that yields no results.

That said, tools like herbs, oils, crystals, and cauldrons can be powerful and fun to use in your spells. Just don't feel pressured or discouraged if you don't have much to start. Keep your magic straightforward and powerful. The right tools and ingredients will come.

"AS ABOVE, SO BELOW"

Tools, ingredients, and symbols are based on the magical theory of sympathetic magic and correspondence. You might hear the phrase, "As Above, So Below," which means the spiritual qualities of objects are passed down to earth. It's "sympathetic magic," or "this equals that," like how a figure of a lion represents that power but is not an actual lion.

Start by following lists, charts, and spells to get a feel for what others use and then begin to discover your own meaningful symbolism and correspondences.

PERMISSION

Spellbooks are like guidelines. They should be modified, simplified, or embellished to your liking. And don't degrade your magic by calling it "lazy." Keeping your witchcraft simple is okay. Go ahead, you have permission.

Also, it's not a competition to see who can use the most esoteric stuff in their spell. Hooray! It's about finding your personal power and style.

SPELLCASTING OUTLINE:
1. Plan and prepare.
2. Cast a circle.
3. Ground and center.
4. Invoke a deity or connection to self.
5. Raise energy.
6. Do your spellcraft (like the spells in this book).
7. Ground and center again.
8. Close your circle.
9. Clean up.
10. Act in accord (and be patient).

1. PLAN AND PREPARE: If you're doing a written spell, read it several times to get familiar with it. Decide if there's anything you'll substitute or change. If you're writing your own spell, enjoy the process and mystery of seeing the messages and theme come together.

Gather all of the items you'll be using (if any) and plan out the space and time where you'll do the spell. Spells can be impromptu, so preparations can be quick and casual if you like.

2. CAST A CIRCLE AND CALL THE QUARTERS: A magic circle is a container to collect the energy of your spell. Circles are also protective, as they form a ring or "barrier" around you. Circles can elevate your space to a higher vibration and clear out unwanted energy before you begin. Calling the Quarters is done to get the universal energies of the elements flowing. Incense is typically burned at the same time to purify the air and energy. If you can't burn things, that's ok. If you've never cast a circle, try it. It's a mystical experience like no other. Once you have a few candles lit and start to walk around it, magic does happen!

HOW TO CAST A CIRCLE: This is a basic, bare-bones way to cast a circle. It's often much more elaborate, and this explanation barely does it justice, so read up to find out more. And note that while some cast the circle first and then call the Quarters, some do it the other way around.

1. Hold out your hand, wand, or crystal, and imagine a white light and a sphere of pure energy surrounding your space, as you circle around clockwise three times. Your circle can be large or it can be tiny, just space for you and your materials.

2: Call the Four Quarters or Five Points of the Pentagram, depending on your preferences. The Quarters (also known as the Elements!) are Earth (North), Air (East), Fire (South), and Water (West). Many use the Pentagram and also call the 5th Element, Spirit or Self.

Face in each direction and say a few words to welcome the element. For example, "To the North, I call upon the power of grounding and strength. To the East, I call upon the source of knowledge. To the South, I call upon the passion and burning desire to take action. To the West, I call upon the intuition of emotion. To Spirit and Source of Self, I call upon guidance and light."

3. GROUND AND CENTER: Grounding and centering prepare you to use the energy from the Earth, elements, and universe. Most witches agree that if you skip these steps, you'll be drawing off of your own energy, which can be exhausting and ineffective. It's wise to ground and center both before and after a spell. It's like the difference between being "plugged into" the magical energy of the Earth and universe versus "draining your batteries."

HOW TO GROUND AND CENTER:
To ground, imagine the energy coming up from the core of the Earth and into your feet, as you breathe deeply. You can visualize deep roots from your feet all the way into the center of the Earth, with these roots drawing the Earth's energy in and out of you. The point is to allow these great channels of energy to flow through you and into your spell. You can also imagine any of your negative energy, thoughts, or stress leaving.

To center, once you've got a good flow of energy from the ground, imagine the energy shining through and out the top of your head as a pure form of your highest creative self and then back in as the light of guidance. Suspend yourself here between the Earth and the sky, supported with the energy flowing freely through you, upheld, balanced, cleansed, and "in flow" with the energy of the universe. This process takes just a couple of minutes.

4. INVOKE A DEITY OR CREATIVE SOURCE: If you'd like to invoke a deity or your highest self to help raise energy and your vibration, call upon them. Invoking deities is way deeper than this book, so research it more if it calls to you!

5. RAISE ENERGY: The point of raising energy is to channel the universal (magical!) forces you tapped into through the previous steps to use in your spell. And raising energy is fun. You can sing, dance, chant, meditate, or do breath work. You want to do something that feels natural, so you can really get into it, lose yourself, and raise your state of consciousness.

A good way to start is to chant "Ong," allowing the roof of your mouth to vibrate ever so slightly. This vibration changes up the energy in your mind, body, and breath and is a simple yet powerful technique.

Another tip is to raise energy to the point of the "peak" where you feel it at its highest. Don't go too far where you start to tucker out or lose enthusiasm!

6. DO YOUR SPELL: Your spell can be as simple as saying an intention and focusing on achieving the outcome of what you want, or it can be more elaborate. Whichever way you prefer, do what feels right to you.

TIPS ON VISUALIZATION AND INTENTION:
Most spellwork involves a bit of imagination and intention, and here are some subtleties you can explore.

The Power of You The most important tool in magic is you. You've got it—both power right now and vast untapped power that you can explore. To cast a successful spell, you've got to focus your mind and genuinely feel the emotions and feelings of the things you want to manifest.

If you haven't started meditating in some form yet, start now! It's not too late, and it's easier than you think.

Visualize the Outcome
Visualization doesn't have to be visual. In fact, *feeling* the outcome of what you want may be more effective than seeing it (try both). And try to feel or see the *completion* of your desire without worrying about the process or *how* you'll get there.

If you don't know how you're going to achieve your goal (yet!), it can feel overwhelming when you try to visualize how you're going to pull it off. Instead, feel the sense of calm, completion, and control that you'll feel *after* you achieve it.

Phrase it Positively
Another tip is to phrase your intentions and desires positively. You're putting energy into this, so make sure the intention is going to be good for you. Instead of saying what you don't want, "to get out of my bad job that I hate," phrase it positively, "I want to do something that's fulfilling with my career."

Then you'll be able to feel good about it as you visualize and cast your spell.

7. GROUND AND CENTER AGAIN

After your spell, it's important to ground out any excess energy. Do this again by visualizing energy flowing through you and out. You can also imagine any "extra" energy you have petering out as you release it back into the Earth.

8. CLOSE YOUR CIRCLE

If you called the Quarters or a deity, let them know the spell has ended by calling them out again, with thanks if desired.

Close your circle the opposite of how you opened it, circling around three times or more counterclockwise. Then say, "This circle is closed," or do a closing chant or song to finish your spell.

9. CLEAN UP

Don't be messy with your magic! Put away all of your spell items.

10. ACT IN ACCORD: Once you have cast your spell, you've got to take action. You can cast a spell to become a marine biologist, but if you don't study for it, it's never going to happen. So take action towards what you want to open the possibility for it to come.

Look for signs, intuition, and coincidences that point you in the direction of your desires. If you get inspired after a spell, take action! Don't be surprised if you ask for money and then come up with a new idea to make money. Follow those clues, especially if they feel exciting and good.

If your spell comes true, discard and "release" any charm bag, poppet, or item you used to hold and amplify energy. Also, give thanks (if that's in your practice) or repay the universe in some way, doing something kind or of service that you feel is a solid trade for what you received from your spell.

WHAT IF YOUR SPELL DOESN'T WORK?

It's true that not all spells will work! But sometimes the results just take longer than you'd like, so be patient.

If your spell doesn't work, you can use divination or meditation to do some digging into reasons why.

The good news is your own magic, power, frequency, and intention is still on your side. You can try again and add more energy in the direction of your desired outcome by casting another spell.

Give it some deep thought. What else is at play? Did you really take inspired action? Are you totally honest with yourself about what you want? Are there any thoughts or feelings about your spell that feel "off"? Are you grateful for what you already have? Can you "give back" or reciprocate with service or energy?

FOR MORE TIPS AND INSPIRATION:

Seek out websites, books, podcasts, and videos on spirituality. Follow your intuition and curiosity to deepen your practice and find your own style. And check out other books in the *Coloring Book of Shadows* series, like the *Book of Spells* and *Witch Life*.

SOUTHERN HEMISPHERE MAGIC

If you're in the Southern Hemisphere in a place like Australia, there are a couple of differences that you'll need to note.

The biggest difference is that since seasonal shifts are opposite on the calendar year, you'll feel the energy of Samhain around May 1 instead of October 31.

Southern Hemisphere "spinning and circle casting" will go "sun wise" according to the south—counterclockwise for invoking (drawing in), clockwise for banishing (letting go).

North and South Elements are also typically swapped in Southern Hemisphere magic—North = Fire, South = Earth.

SO MOTE IT BE.

About the Artist

Amy Cesari

and her familiars Mr. Toad & Merlin

Amy is an author and illustrator who loves animated musicals. She also likes watercolor painting, witchcraft, and walking on the beach in a really big sun hat.

Not only does she own every Nintendo game console ever made, she's earned several fancy diplomas and enjoys continued studies in various magical practices.

CONTACT AMY AND GET YOURSELF SOME BOOKS & MAGICAL FREEBIES AT:
Amy@ColoringBookofShadows.com
ColoringBookofShadows.com

©2025 Amy Cesari, Book of Shadows LLC

LOVE THIS BOOK?!
THERE'S MORE!

SHOP.COLORINGBOOKOFSHADOWS.COM

Coloring Books:

   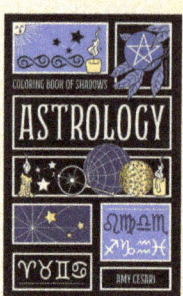

Full-Color Books:

THANK YOU!

Bollank
Art Production
& Color Assistant

Wendy Ledger
Editor
WendyLedgerAuthor.com

Fiona Horne
Editor of Magick
& Editor
FionaHorne.com

Cora Spring Moon
Editor